To: _____

From: _____

Date: _____

Bible Stories
Old Testament

Illustrated by Sam Butcher

Baker Books
A Division of Baker Book House Co
Grand Rapids, Michigan 49516

Art © 1979, 1981, 1987, 1996 by Precious Moments, Inc.
Text © 1999 by Baker Book House

Published by Baker Books
a division of Baker Book House Company
P.O. Box 6287, Grand Rapids, MI 49516-6287

Printed in the United States of America

ISBN 0-8010-4427-8

Library of Congress Cataloging-in-Publication Data is on file at the Library of Congress, Washington, D.C.

For current information about all releases from Baker Book House, visit our web site:

http://www.bakerbooks.com

List of Stories

Jacob's Dream

Genesis 28:10–22

Jacob's parents told him to find a wife in a faraway city. So Jacob left home to obey them. When it got dark Jacob stopped to rest for the night. He used a stone for a pillow and lay down to sleep. Soon he began to dream.

In his dream Jacob saw a stairway coming down from the sky. Angels were going up and down the stairs, and God was standing at the top with a special message for Jacob.

God told Jacob that he would have a huge family with lots of children, grandchildren, great-grandchildren, and even great-great-grandchildren. In fact, there would be too many to count! God promised to watch over Jacob's family wherever they went.

After the dream Jacob was surprised (and a little scared), because he knew that God was there with him. In the morning Jacob took his stone pillow and set it up to mark the place where God had talked to him. He called the spot Bethel.

Just as God made a promise to Jacob, Jacob promised God something too. He said he would worship and serve God. And he did! Later God changed Jacob's name to Israel. The Israelites, everyone in Jacob's big family, were known as God's people. And God kept his promise to watch over Jacob and his family.

Joseph Becomes a Slave

Genesis 37:12–36

Joseph was Jacob's favorite son, and that made his brothers angry! They were jealous because their father had given Joseph a special coat. And they didn't like it when Joseph told them about his dreams where everyone bowed down to him. In fact, they hated Joseph!

One day Jacob asked Joseph to check on his brothers in the field. When they saw him coming, Joseph's brothers decided they should kill him. But first they made fun of his dreams and tried to scare him.

Joseph's oldest brother, Reuben, didn't want Joseph to be killed. So he told the others to throw Joseph into a deep, dark pit instead. Reuben thought he could come back later to take Joseph home.

The brothers took Joseph's special coat away from him and then did what Reuben said. They threw him in a pit. But Reuben's plan to help Joseph didn't work. Some strangers came by on their way to a different country, and Reuben's brothers sold Joseph to them for some money. So the strangers took Joseph away to be a slave. The brothers put some goat's blood on Joseph's coat to make their father think that Joseph was dead.

But God took care of Joseph, even in a faraway land. He made him an important man who saved many people. And later, Joseph's brothers even bowed down to him, just as he had dreamed!

Baby Moses
Exodus 2:1–10

When Moses was born the Israelites were living in the land of Egypt. The king of Egypt was worried about having too many Israelites in his country, so he made a law that said every new Israelite baby boy was to be thrown into the river.

But Moses' mother wouldn't let anyone hurt her baby. She kept him a secret for three months—until he was too big to hide. Then she made a waterproof basket and used it to let Moses float in the Nile River. Moses'

sister, Miriam, watched to see what would happen.

Miriam saw the king's daughter come to take a bath in the river. When the princess discovered the basket, she opened it and saw that the baby was crying. The princess was sad for Moses and wanted to help him.

Miriam had an idea about how to keep her brother with her family. She asked the princess, "Would you like me to find a woman to take care of the baby for you?" When the princess said yes, Miriam went to find her mother. The princess hired Moses' mother to take care of him!

When Moses was old enough he went to live in the king's palace. He grew up as the king's grandson! And God made Moses a great leader for the people. Many years later he led God's people out of Egypt.

Joshua's Words from God

Joshua 1:1–9

Joshua looked at the land on the other side of the Jordan River from where he and the other Israelites were camped. Their great leader, Moses, had just died, and now God was speaking to Joshua about what the people needed to do.

God told Joshua to be strong and brave. He promised to help the people cross the river and go into the land if they listened to him. Joshua didn't need to be afraid of anyone or anything, because God

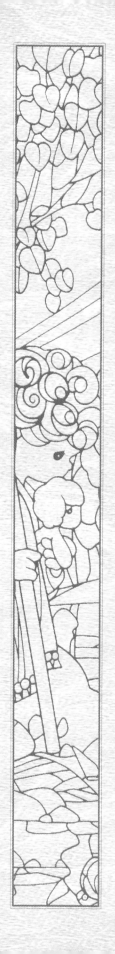

promised to be with him wherever he went.

So Joshua told the people to get ready to cross the river. He reminded them of God's promise to give them a special land and told them that now was the time when God would give it to them. The people knew that Joshua was the new leader God had picked for them, and they listened to him just as they had followed Moses.

God helped Joshua lead the Israelites into the land of Canaan. And God kept his promise to stay with them. By doing what God told them to do, the people won every battle. God even made the walls of a big city come tumbling down for them!

Ruth Stays with Naomi
Ruth 1:1–19

Ruth loved her husband and her husband's family. They had come to Ruth's country from Judah. Soon after they arrived her husband's father died. A few years later Ruth's husband and his brother died. Now her mother-in-law, Naomi, was left alone. She had no husband or sons anymore. So she decided to return to her home country.

Ruth and her sister-in-law Orpah helped Naomi pack her things and started to travel with her. But Naomi

told them to go back to their parents' homes. They both told Naomi that they wanted to go with her. Naomi was thankful for their kindness to her, but she wanted them to go back to their homes so they could find new husbands.

Orpah finally agreed to go back, but Ruth said she would stay with Naomi no matter what happened. Ruth showed her love for Naomi when she promised to make Naomi's home her home and to worship Naomi's God.

So the two women traveled together to the city of Bethlehem.

When they arrived, God rewarded Ruth for staying with Naomi. Ruth met a new husband who took care of her and Naomi. And her great-grandson David became one of Israel's greatest kings.

Hannah's Prayer

1 Samuel 1:1–28

Hannah was so happy to have her son, Samuel. God had given him to her, and now she was going to give him back to God.

Before Samuel was born Hannah was very sad because she did not have any children. One time when Hannah and her husband were at the temple, Hannah was so sad that she was crying while she prayed to God. Eli the priest thought something was wrong with her; she was moving her

lips, but her voice wasn't making any sound!

When Eli asked her about it, Hannah told him about her prayer. She said she had promised God that if he would let her have a baby boy, she would bring the boy back to live in the temple and serve God. Eli saw that she was telling the truth, and he told her to believe that God would answer her prayer.

God did answer Hannah's prayer for a baby boy! And Hannah kept her promise. She brought Samuel to live

in the temple with Eli where he
would grow up to be a great leader
in the land of Israel. God used
Hannah's son to teach the people
about his promises.

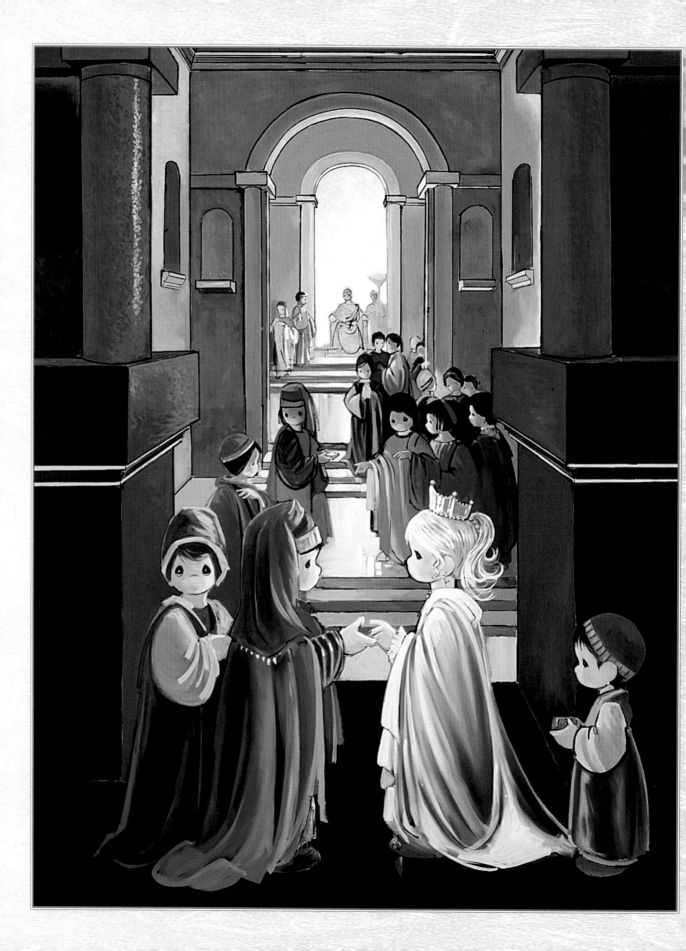

Esther Defends Her People

Esther 4–8

Queen Esther knew she had to save her people. Her uncle had told her about Haman's evil plan to kill all the Jews. But Esther knew it was going to be dangerous to ask King Xerxes for help. He didn't even know that Esther was a Jew!

Esther asked her uncle to have all of the Jews pray for her. Then she went to find the king. The laws in Esther's country said that anyone who came to the king without being asked for could be killed. But Esther knew God was with her.

Instead of being angry, the king was happy to see her. He agreed to come to a special meal Esther planned for him and Haman. After the meal, Esther asked them to come back for another special dinner the next day. When they did, she told the king about Haman's wicked plan. The king was very angry at Haman for trying to hurt Queen Esther's people.

To protect the Jews, the king gave them special permission to fight against anyone who attacked them. So because Esther was brave and trusted God to help her talk to the king, her people were saved.